DRESSAGE BASICS

Outlined Step By Step

SANDY JACOBSEN

DRESSAGE BASICS
OUTLINED STEP BY STEP

A "take to the stable" quick reference guide for the beginning dressage rider by SANDY JACOBSEN.

Copyright© 1997 by Sandy Jacobsen
Library of Congress Catalog Card No. 97-93044
ISBN No. 0-9656637-0-1

2nd printing 1998

Published by Langfield Press
        21680 McGilvray Rd.
        Bend, OR 97702

Printed in the United States by
Maverick Publications, Inc.
Bend, Or 97701

NOTES

Use this section for your progress comments or highlights from clinics and lessons.

_____
_____
_____
_____
_____
_____
_____
_____
_____
_____
_____
_____
_____
_____
_____
_____
_____
_____
_____
_____
_____
_____
_____
_____
_____
_____
_____

TABLE OF CONTENTS

ACKNOWLEDGMENT

This book is for my students. They have all given me something in return for the information I gave them. When they get a movement right, the glow on their faces and the excitement in their voices is a great reward.

They are always telling me how hard it is to remember everything I say. They also complain that they can't do everything I tell them to do at once. When they forget one critical component of a movement, of course it doesn't work. I worked hard to teach them and I want to make sure they never forget.

This book is designed to be taken to the stable, set on the rail, and used to refresh your memory as you are riding. Each section has a quick reference guide for this purpose. It is also printed in large type so you can read it. So go out there, get on your horse, and have fun.

INTRODUCTION

Dressage is a symphony and poetry in movement expressing the harmony between horse and rider. Except for the sound of rhythmic hoof beats and breath, it is a silent but incredibly fantastic sight to the eyes of the viewer. Seemingly effortless for both horse and rider, is the deception of many messages being transmitted between the two.

Sounds pretty hokey, huh? But on those days when you ride correctly and your horse responds perfectly, it feels just like that. The spectator watching a talented dressage horse/rider combination is fascinated by the grace and beauty. Dressage is great for the people who ride it, but how do you become one of them? Many people are intimidated by dressage and think it too complicated. Not so, as it is natural for the horse. There is a challenge for the rider, but that is the fun.

Learning dressage is like learning a new language. At first everything is Greek and you don't even speak; you have to use your hands and legs to communicate. Furthermore, you are asked to do one thing with the left hand, something else with the right, AND, at the same time, move your leg. This is overload; that requires coordination. How are you ever going to be able to do it?

The answer is -- one step at a time. Because you bought this book, you are now ahead of the game. This book is designed to give you a mental and visual picture of dressage basics. The basics of dressage are the foundation for your building blocks as you progress in this sport. Without a solid foundation, in time, your building will crumble. No one starts dressage at Grand Prix, just as one cannot sit down to a piano for the first time and play Bach. Start simply and work your way up, such as learning all your movements at the walk. It is easy to keep your balance and use your aids properly. The horse will also be able to understand what you ask him to do.

A numerical quick reference follows each section of this book for your convenience. Follow the quick reference guides in the numerical order given. This step by step approach to dressage will simplify your learning process and give you a great foundation.

Please read the glossary before going on to the main text. Everything will make a lot more sense. Each major section of the book is coded on the right margin for your convenience. Use these codes to immediately turn to the section of the book you wish to refer.

GLOSSARY
(GREEK TRANSLATED)

ABOVE THE BIT - Occurs when the horse raises his head or extends his nose and is no longer moving through the top of his neck.

AIDS - The rider's communication tools used to control and direct the horse. There are five aids - two hands, two legs, and the rider's seat.

BALANCE - The rider's ability to stay centered properly on the horse. It also includes staying with the horse's motion.

BEHIND THE BIT - (Behind vertical) An evasion or resistance to the bit. The horse or the rider pulls his nose back behind a vertical line running from forehead to nose. The horse may also be too low in the poll.

BEND - The horse curves his spine from ear to tail. The bend enables the horse to be better balanced and athletic while circling or turning. Bending also helps the horse to achieve more engagement of his inside hind leg in lateral movements.

CHANGE OF REIN - When the rider changes direction she must also change to a new outside rein. This is generally performed on the diagonal.

CIRCLE - A very common movement used to help the horse learn to engage by stepping under with his inside hind leg. The circle also shows the horse's ability to bend and stay on the aids.

COLLECTION - The horse in self-carriage with added engagement, impulsion, and suspension. The horse's frame is shorter and haunches are lower with a stride that shortens in length because it increases height.

CONSISTENT - Applying aids or performing a movement in the exact same way.

CONTACT - A consistent feel of the bit through the reins. This feel should be elastic and soft. It is like lightly hanging your fingers on the reins to ensure they stay taught.

CROOKED - When moving in a circle or straight line, the horse's hind feet do not follow in the tracks of the front feet. The horse's hip or shoulder could be off track.

DIAGONAL AIDS - Using one hand and one leg from opposite sides together. An example is the inside leg working with the outside rein.

DIRECT REIN - Using a rein aid to encourage the horse to flex his head and neck to the direction he is being asked to move.

DOWN TRANSITION - Changing the horse's gait to a slower movement as in canter to trot or trot to walk.

DRIVING AIDS - The legs and the seat are the rider's driving (forward) aids.

ELASTICITY - Freedom and ease of movement without resistance or tension.

ENGAGEMENT - Stepping under with the hind legs combined with extra flexion of the hock and the stifle which lowers the haunches. The horse also must be on the bit, in self-carriage, and going forward.

FADE IN OR OUT - The hip or shoulder of the horse does not stay on track. The horse escapes through or ignores the rider's aids.

FALL ON FOREHAND - The horse loses its balance during a down transition and does not remain in self-carriage. A horse on the forehand is not stepping under behind and is carrying too much weight in front.

FEEL - The rider's ability to sense the motion and position of the horse through touch using her five aids.

FLEXION - The supple bending of the horse's various body parts. (Poll, neck, back, hock, etc.)

FOLLOWING - The rider moving in unison with the horse's motion.

FORWARD - Free, energetic and relaxed motion that is not hurried.

GOING THROUGH - The horse's hind legs are stepping well underneath with energy that is traveling up to the back, forward through the top of the neck, and on the bit. Resistance or tension will block this energy that goes from the hind legs to the bit.

HALF-HALT - The combination of hand, leg, and seat aids momentarily blocking and then driving the horse forward to gain attention and added engagement.

HANDS - Two of the rider's five aids. A very important communication tool that is generally misused. The hands should be quiet and relaxed with elastic fingers.

IMPULSION - The energetic forward thrust of the horse created by reaching under with his hind legs.

INDIRECT REIN - Using a rein aid to encourage the horse to flex his head and neck to the opposite direction he is being asked to move.

INSIDE LEG OR REIN - When riding a circle or turn there will always be an inside and outside of the movement. It is generally easier to think of in and out rather than left and right.

LATERAL MOVEMENT - Specific movements where the horse crosses his legs moving sideways or on three tracks. His hind feet do not follow the steps of his front feet. An example is leg yield or shoulder-in.

LEG - The area of a rider's leg from the top of the calf to the inside heel. Driving aids sending the horse forward or sideways.

LEG YIELD - A movement in which the horse moves forward and sideways at the same time, keeping his body parallel to the track. The horse should cross both front and hind legs. It is used to teach the horse engagement and suppleness.

ON THE AIDS - A horse in a correct frame, moving with impulsion, that is responsive to the rider's aids.

ON THE BIT - The horse is moving freely forward with total acceptance of the bit and the rein contact. The horse must have enough impulsion to step under behind so he can carry himself and remain balanced.

OUTSIDE LEG - See "inside leg."

RELAXATION - A horse or rider that is free of tension and is not nervous.

RESISTANCE - A horse expressing apprehension or refusing to respond to the rider's aids.

RHYTHM - Consistent, even strides made by the horse. The strides should be the same length and move at the same speed.

SEAT - One of the rider's five aids. The seat is influenced by the position and weight of the upper body. It can be used for blocking or driving the horse's motion.

SELF-CARRIAGE - The horse moving in a balanced and correct frame, who is not relying on support from the rider.

SHOULDER-FORE - An engagement and suppling movement used to teach the horse to move from the inside leg to the outside rein. This movement is also used to begin teaching the horse shoulder-in.

SHOULDER-IN - A lateral movement in which the horse moves forward with a bending frame making three tracks. It is used to teach the horse engagement and suppleness.

STRAIGHT - Moving in a line with the hind feet stepping directly behind the front feet.

STRETCH - A relaxed horse moving freely and willingly, extending his legs and neck.

SUPPLE - A horse responding to the rider's aids without any resistance or tension when asked to flex and bend.

SUSPENSION - A horse traveling with moments when all four feet are off the ground between steps. The horse's stride length shortens because the height increases. The horse appears to be floating in air between steps.

TEMPO - The speed with which the horse is moving.

TRACK UP - The hind feet land in the print of the front feet.

TRANSITION - The change from one gait to another, or altering a gait such as a collected trot to an extended trot.

TURN ON FOREHAND - A movement where the horse steps sideways, crossing his hind feet one in front of the other, while the front feet move in place and slightly step forward. It is used to teach the horse engagement and suppleness.

UP TRANSITION - Changing the horse's gait to a faster movement as in walk to trot or trot to canter.

1. WHAT MAKES A GOOD DRESSAGE HORSE?

Above all, be realistic about your ability, desire, and dedication; as well as the horse's potential for the level of dressage performance you want the horse to attain. Regardless of their desire, not all people are natural riders and good horse communicators. You must be capable of relaxing, keeping your emotions in check, and having lots of patience.

Likewise, not all horses have an exceptional mental and physical capacity for dressage. Some breeds, because of temperament and conformation, are more suitable and will progress further. The best dressage horses have conformation that will allow them to carry a dressage frame correctly and perform the movements easily. The dressage horse should have:

1. Uphill conformation with his withers level with or above his hip.
2. Large, well-sloped shoulder that is very free moving.
3. Medium to long neck that comes out of the top of his shoulder.
4. Thin throat latch.
5. Medium to short and very strong back with a good set of withers.
6. Long, sloping hip with enough substance to carry his (and your) weight.
7. Strong hocks with good flexion.
8. Good bone and soundness.
9. Short cannon bones.
10. Long, sloping pasterns.
11. Round, well-formed hooves.

Even more important than the horse's physical capability is his mental capacity for dressage. The dressage horse should be:

1. Energetic without being tense.
2. Able to relax and move freely without stiffness.
3. Attentive to you and not what's going on around him.
4. Forgiving.
5. Giving and capable of putting out extra effort without arguing.
6. Capable of not anticipating and reacting to every move you make.

Almost every horse and rider can perform dressage. The level of performance is the only limit. This level will be determined by desire, mental and physical ability, time, and money. Before any horse can be asked the basic movements of dressage, he must have RELAXATION, DESIRE TO GO FORWARD, and SUBMISSION, always in this order.

2. BASIC REQUIREMENTS FOR DRESSAGE

RELAXATION

Relaxation in the horse is an attentive, quiet, and supple demeanor. Lack of relaxation is attributed to basically two things -- tension or excess energy. You need to decide which is the problem before seeking a solution.

Tension could be caused by unfamiliar surroundings. Walk the horse around for a while and let him get a good look at things. If this is a common problem, try to take him to other stables and riding areas every week. Some horses have strong herd instincts and don't deal well with being separated from horses in the warm-up area. Horses can also attach themselves to a buddy. Practice separating a dependent horse and get him to focus on his work by using consistent, firm aids. Some horses have to be separated from buddies by stabling them in different aisles at shows.

Another cause of tension can come directly from you. Horses tend to mirror the emotions of the rider. If you are stiff and tight, the horse will be too. If you are frightened or nervous, the horse can interpret your emotion as something that could hurt him and react with tension.

Tension also can be caused by improperly fitting equipment. Check the bridle, pad, and saddle to be sure the horse is comfortable. Inexpensive or old equipment generally is not advisable. The horse will not be comfortable and you will have difficulty sitting correctly. Properly fitting equipment for the horse and rider is well worth the effort and expense.

If excess energy is your problem, try longeing the horse before riding. It could be that the horse needs turn out time if he is kept in a stall. He may be going stir-crazy.

An abundance of energy can also be caused by diet. Horses only need 9 - 12% protein. A diet of higher protein levels can cause the horse to be very energetic. Read the ingredients in your feed and be careful of the combinations you feed. Ask your hay dealer for a protein analysis of your hay. Some alfalfa can be near 20% protein, which can cause excess energy and other problems.

However you accomplish it, be sure the horse is relaxed. Lack of relaxation will prevent the horse from moving freely forward and will hinder submission. A tense or energetic horse will also have difficulty concentrating on you and responding to your aids.

If the horse will not relax he may need:

1. More time to gain confidence in strange surroundings and separation from buddies.
2. Trust in his rider.
3. Correct and comfortable equipment for the horse and rider.
4. Longeing to take the edge off.
5. Change to a lower protein diet.

DESIRE TO GO FORWARD

The horse who is exhibiting a desire to go forward appears to be enjoying his work. He should reach freely forward with his forearms and shoulders. The hind legs should step well underneath and over the front hoof print. Ideally, there should be a swing to his gait and a spring to his step.

The energy and speed with which he moves (impulsion) should be active, but not hurried. Some horses are just naturally lazy. You may have to convince the horse that you desire more ambition from him by using spurs or a whip to encourage him. Be careful not to abuse or overly intimidate the horse, because he may get tense which will inhibit his forward motion.

The horse also has to be in appropriate physical condition for the work you are asking him to do. Some horses have physical limitations and are not capable of big, swinging, springy strides. Do not ask the horse for more than he is able to deliver.

If the horse is not willing to go forward you may need to:

1. Use a whip or spurs if he is lazy or ignoring your aids.
2. Reestablish relaxation because a tense horse does not go forward.
3. Check his physical condition.
4. Be aware of the horse's natural conformation limitations.

SUBMISSION

Submission is the willingness of the horse to respond quickly and correctly to your aids. Horses should move away from pressure whether it is from your hand, leg, or seat. If the horse does not respond to your aids, he is said to be resistant. It is usually not the horse's fault when he exhibits resistance. There are many causes for the lack of submission. A lot of care and thought must be given to submission, as it is the most difficult aspect of dressage to achieve.

The rider is generally the greatest cause for resistance in the horse. Tension, lack of balance, inconsistency, and improper use of aids can all cause resistance. Correct position and consistent, sympathetic use of aids are generally the best answer to gaining submission. Be sure to maintain relaxation, reward the horse for correct movements, reprimand him for resistance, and repeat your aids for a movement until it is performed correctly. If the horse is uncomfortable with your equipment, or his own physical condition, he may exhibit resistance.

If the horse is not submissive to your hand or leg you may need to:

1. Ensure your position is correct, and your aids are consistent and sympathetic.
2. Stop and repeat your aids for problems.
3. Maintain relaxation, praise the horse for correct response, and reprimand him for resistance.
4. Try other equipment. (Bits, pads, saddles, etc.)
5. Longe in side reins or ride with draw reins.
6. Assess the horse's physical condition.

3. EFFECTIVE AIDS

The key to sending the horse forward and getting submission is use of effective aids. Your aids are the communication tools to control and direct the horse. An aid is only effective if the horse responds to it correctly. In dressage you have five aids -- two hands, two legs, and your seat in combination with your back. You must sit in the correct position so your aids can be applied to the proper area on the horse.

Figure 1 (Pg. 29) explains the proper position for each part of your body. Periodically make a check of your body parts to be sure everything is in its proper place.

Figure 2 (Pg. 30) shows the effects of not staying centered on the horse. Some riders are physically misaligned and do not sit straight even though they feel they are. Have a ground person check your position so you can determine if what you feel is correct.

Figure 3 (Pg. 31) exhibits the importance of keeping your shoulders back. All beginning riders want to do the same things that are natural for a person, but wrong for the horse. Leaning forward (whether a fetal position or a misguided attempt to help the horse move forward) is one of the most common mistakes.

Three things must happen in order for an aid to be effective -- POSITION, BALANCE, and RESPONSE.

POSITION

HEAD

Your head is not an aid, but does play an important role in balance and direction. Keeping your chin up will encourage erect shoulders and a strong back. This will help lighten the horse's front end and make your seat aid more effective. Be careful not to tip your head to one side. It will cause you to displace your ribs to the other side and possibly drop your shoulder (Fig. 2, Pg. 30).

EYES

Your eyes must look in the direction you intend to go. Your eyes precede and influence body motion which directly influences the horse. The turning of your head to look right will be felt by the horse, and he will begin preparing for movement to the right.

SHOULDERS

Your shoulders are very important to the balance of both you and the horse, because of the amount of weight in this part of your body. Your shoulders should be above your hip with your chest raised, and held in place by your stomach muscles. Be careful not to raise your shoulders where your arms are attached. Think tall and stretch through your spine. Imagine having a space between each rib. If your shoulders come in front of the vertical, you will tip the horse's balance and weight onto his forehand (Fig. 3, Pg. 31). Your shoulder position directly influences the effectiveness of your seat aid. The horse moves with a center of motion which can be depicted as a vertical line going up from the horse's withers. If you tip in front of that line, you are in front of or ahead of the horse and cannot send the horse forward correctly. In down transitions, half-halts, and halts, your shoulders can be taken a tiny bit behind vertical. This will enhance your seat aid and help prevent loss of balance.

Proper position of your upper body will greatly increase your strength. If your back is flat and your shoulders are above or slightly behind your hip; and the horse pulls on you or is resistant in his head, his pull will deepen your seat and help send him forward. This leverage advantage gives you a great deal of strength without creating any tension in your muscles (Fig. 3).

Think of holding the reins with your shoulders rather than with your hands, elbows, and forearms. Holding the reins with your elbows and forearms will create tension. Since your shoulders hold your hands, your shoulders must be steady and kept in place. Moving your shoulders forward or back can add or subtract an inch from the rein length. This motion creates a change in contact and makes it difficult for the horse to stay on the bit. A clever horse very quickly discovers where you are sitting, and determines what he can or cannot get away with.

Another common fault involving your shoulders is to drop one (Fig. 2). This especially happens when circling or turning the horse. Do not fall into the habit of helping the horse turn by leaning to the inside. Dropping your inside shoulder not only unbalances the horse, but causes your hip to slide off center on the saddle making your seat aid ineffective. Try to move your inside shoulder back to match the shoulder angle of the horse (Fig. 7, Pg. 62).

22

ELBOWS

Your elbows should be held close and just in front of the center of your side. If your elbows are too far forward with little flexion, your arms and hands will be stiff. Elbows coming behind the center of your side will result in your hands being less effective, more constricted, and will encourage your shoulders to round and come forward. Your elbows must be bent and your hands low enough to create a straight line from the bit to your elbow.

Several parts of your body are hinges and shock absorbers. Your elbows are hinges with an angle that opens and closes. Your elbows will move forward and back from your body when the horse walks and canters as he nods his head.

ARMS AND HANDS

With your shoulders relaxed and in the correct position, your arms and hands can achieve communication through the reins. Steady hands are crucial for the horse to have a steady head. Acceptance of the bit is also directly related to steady hands. Relaxation of your elbows and forearms is the key to good hands. Your hands have very little movement other than following the natural flow and rhythm of the horse.

Your hands are held close together, level and lower than your elbows, forming the same shape as the withers. Your hands stay close to the withers (about 1") with one hand on each side, almost never crossing over. Your hands mostly move forward and back following the rein motion as the neck flexes with the bend. Imagine tying a

23

6" piece of string between your hands and then tying the middle of the string to the horse's mane. Your hands should stay within this parameter unless you are riding a very green horse or have extreme resistance. (Never actually tie your hands together, only imagine.) One experiment you can try is to put on fluorescent orange gloves to see how obvious your hand motion is.

Your wrists remain flat with very little flexion, maintaining a straight line from your elbow to the bit. Your thumb holds the rein against your index finger so your ring finger can be flexible for softening. Your fingers hold the rein twice; once between your thumb and index finger, and second between your ring finger and little finger.

Although hands should be the least used of all aids, they are unfortunately the most abused aid. Stiff forearms and hands restrict the horse's motion. Everything your hands do goes immediately down the reins to the horse's mouth. Stiff hands are like static electricity going through the reins.

Your hands must be relaxed, without tension, so they can flow with the horse's motion. To help your hands remain relaxed, try to hold them in place with your shoulders -- not with your elbows or forearms. The feeling in your forearms and hands should be that of holding a tray in which items would slide off the front rather than stay on. Don't hold your tray up or you will create tension in your forearms and hands.

While your hands must be quiet, they should not be dead. Your fingers must be alive and elastic. Fingers should open and close, creating squeezes or vibrations which will massage and finesse the horse's jaw into relaxation (softening).

If your hands and shoulders are staying in the correct position, you could still be missing an important part of a correct head and neck position for the horse. If the reins are not the same length, the horse will have trouble with balance, and this can cause you to be out of position. Reins that are too short can cause you to reach too far forward, have your elbows too straight, or tip your shoulders forward. Reins that are too long can cause you to bring your elbows too far back and tip your shoulders forward.

Use reins with stops sewn on or wrap electrical tape evenly along the reins where you hold them. This will ensure that you have the correct length for each rein, and that you are consistent with your rein length for each gait. The rein stops also help you hold on to the reins without tensing your hands.

WAIST

The waist is your shock absorber to soften the bounce of the horse. It is like a wedge of firm foam rubber deflecting the motion of the hip as it follows the horse's motion. A relaxed waist prevents your shoulders from rebounding off your hip. This is important because your shoulders hold your hands. Stretching through your waist area will help with elasticity. The stretching is done with your stomach muscles. Strong stomach muscles aid a strong back and enable you to carry your shoulders.

A flexible waist is also necessary for moving your inside shoulder back when circling or turning the horse. You will need to twist in your waist as your shoulders turn the opposite direction of your hip (Fig. 7, Pg. 62).

SEAT

Your seat is a very important aid in dressage and must be centered in the deepest part of the saddle, with even pressure on each side. Your pelvis should be level to create even pressure on both sides of the saddle. Many women have curved spines, which can cause your pelvis to be tilted. The result is added pressure on one side of the saddle and one leg hanging longer. Keeping your hips centered on the saddle can also be a problem. A quick x-ray by your physician or chiropractor can easily determine if a tilted pelvis is the cause of your problem. The top of your pelvis should be tipped back instead of forward as in hunt seat.

To make your seat effective, it must be relaxed, supple, and consistently deep in the saddle. You cannot influence the horse if your weight is not in the saddle. Tight knees and thighs will reduce the effectiveness of your seat. Also, be sure you are not putting weight in your irons. Your seat can enhance your leg aid by sitting deeper on one side to help move the horse's back laterally. The motion of your body can be used as an aid by activating or deactivating your seat. Blocking or stopping the motion of your seat will cause the horse to momentarily hesitate, balance, and reorganize for down transitions and half-halts. Deepening your seat with the weight of your upper body directly above your hip will send the horse forward.

LEG

Your legs should be kept relaxed and stretched down and long, with no gripping of your knees or thighs.

26

Your lower legs are the most important and most used aid. For clarification, whenever I refer to legs in this book, I am referring the area from the upper calf to the inside heel. Your upper calves should remain in continuous contact with the horse at least touching his hair. Think of your legs as a wet wash cloth draped on the horse's side.

Your feet should be parallel to the horse with your heels slightly lower than your toes. The inside of your heels can be used to emphasize an aid. The back of your heels (which holds the spur) is not an aid. The spur is only used to punish the horse for not listening to the inside of your heels. Your heels must be under your hip in order to apply your leg aid to the proper area of the horse's side. This will be discussed in greater detail later in Response.

1. Keep your head straight with your chin up and look where you want to go.
2. Center your shoulders above your hip and never tip forward.
3. Use your stomach muscles to hold your chest up and keep your shoulders back.
4. Think of holding the reins with your shoulders rather than your elbows and forearms.
5. Place your elbows just in front of the center of your side.
6. Relax your elbows so they can act as a hinge to follow the horse's natural head and neck motion.
7. Keep your wrists flat and form a straight line from elbow to bit.
8. Steady your hands; this is crucial for your horse to have a steady head.

9. Keep your hands close to the withers, one on each side, and mostly move them forward and back.

10. Use alive, elastic fingers to finesse the horse's jaw into relaxation.

11. Be sure the reins are the same length and the correct length for each gait.

12. Supple your waist to prevent your shoulders from rebounding off your hip.

13. Center your seat in the deepest part of the saddle.

14. Use the motion and weight of your upper body (mostly hip) through your seat to block the horse's motion or drive him forward.

15. Stretch your legs down and long.

16. Do not grip with your knees or thighs.

17. Remember "Leg" is the area from your upper calf to your inside heel.

18. Keep your feet parallel to the horse, your heels lower than your toes, and your heels under your hip.

RIDER POSITION

HEAD is level and straight.

EYES are up and looking forward to where you are going.

SHOULDERS are level and directly above your hip with no slouch for a flat back. Stretch your chest up with firm stomach muscles.

ARMS are relaxed with your elbows in front of the center of your side. Be sure your elbows are flexible and your forearms are free of tension.

HANDS should be held lower than your elbows with your thumbs up and slightly in. Keep both hands level, with one hand on each side of the horse's neck. Your fingers should be elastic and soft.

HIPS should be level with even side pressure and centered in the deepest part of the saddle. Your hip must be relaxed and move with the horse.

THIGHS should be stretched down and long. Relax your knees and thighs and do not grip.

LEGS comprise your upper calf to inside heel. Your calf should rest lightly against the horse's side. Legs are the driving and navigation aids for communication with the horse.

HEELS are to be kept under your hip and slightly lower than your toe.

Figure 1

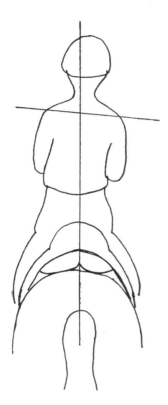 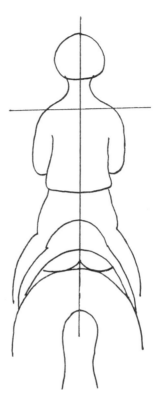

An example of a dropped shoulder causing your hip to be offset.

Correct position with level shoulders and hip centered in the saddle.

Figure 2

RIDER LEVERAGE

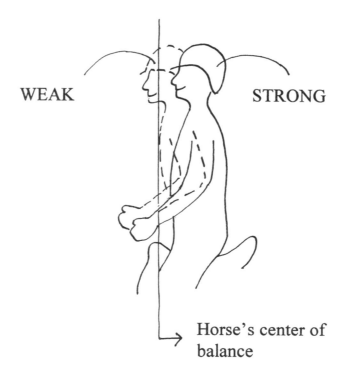

WEAK   STRONG

Horse's center of balance

Pulling your elbows behind the center of your side and tipping your shoulders forward greatly weakens your position. This weakened position prevents you from using your seat aid effectively and can cause you to have tension in your arms. If the horse pulls on your hands, he will pull your seat out of the saddle; but with your shoulders above your hip, pulling by the horse will deepen your seat, giving you leverage that will make your aids more effective.

Figure 3

BALANCE

Proper position must be maintained at all times, which requires good balance. Good balance is crucial to applying and maintaining effective aids. If you lose your balance, you will not be able to apply aids consistently with proper pressure, and to the proper area of the horse.

There is no substitute for many hours in the saddle, but make them constructive hours. The phrase "perfect practice makes perfect" definitely applies to dressage. To maintain balance, try to stay in position by doing a mental checklist of where your body parts are. Feel where your elbows, hands, head, shoulders, etc., are and what they are doing.

Another helpful step is to prepare well for transitions. Plan ahead; know here you are going and what you will do next. Use your mind to envision going to a specific place and what you will do there. Mentally ride ahead of your horse. Do not follow him as a passenger.

Changes in a gait (transitions) are when riders most frequently lose balance. Balance can be greatly improved by riding on the longe. The horse should be steady, well schooled, and dependable. There are many exercises to help you improve position and balance while on the longe, but concentration will help the most. Use riding on the longe to help you feel the horse's motion and rhythm. Concentrate on the horse's foot fall and the motion of his hips and shoulders without looking at them.

Keeping your balance is also necessary to help the horse balance, because if you lose balance, so will the horse. When the horse loses balance, ensure you are in position, and half-halt to help the horse regain balance.

Another aspect of being balanced is to become part of the horse. Try to follow the motion and rhythm of the horse, so the two of you move together as one unit. There is a lot of weight in your upper body, which can greatly affect the horse's balance. Your head and shoulders do not follow the horse's motion, and should stay centered above the horse to help him maintain his balance. Your hands and legs follow and move in rhythm with the horse. Your hip does most of the work to follow the motion of the horse. Because the horse moves his body differently for each gait, he will cause you to move differently in the saddle. As the horse moves, he goes up and down as well as sideways. You must move in the same direction at the same time to stay with the horse.

Relaxation, as previously discussed, is the key to being able to move with the horse. If you tighten your muscles and become stiff, the horse will actually cause you to bounce more.

1. Stay relaxed.
2. Make a checklist of your body parts -- elbows, feet, hands, head, legs, and shoulders. Are you in the correct position?
3. Plan ahead with a consistent preparation for movements.
4. Be extra careful to maintain balance during transitions.
5. Follow the motion and rhythm of the horse.

RESPONSE

An effective aid is one given correctly by you, which gets the correct response from the horse. Regardless of how great your position and how well you keep your balance, your aids are not effective if the horse does not respond appropriately. Measure the appropriate response according to the horse's mental and physical capabilities. Determine his attention span and boredom level so you know how long he is capable of constructively learning. Be realistic about the horse's physical ability and endurance. Do not ask for something he cannot deliver.

Aids must be applied in the correct area on the horse with the correct amount of pressure. The correct area of the horse where you apply an aid should not vary, but the amount of pressure required for a response may vary according to the sensitivity of the horse. For this section we are going to assume you have a correctly trained horse with average sensitivity.

Since aids are communication tools for influencing the horse, you need to know what they should tell the horse. The rider's five aids have specific jobs and should get the following responses.

SHOULDER/SEAT

Your shoulders, back, and seat work together as an aid. Basically the aid is the weight of your upper body used to influence the horse. Your seat aid can be used as a block, such as in half-halt. A horse and rider are hopefully moving forward together at the same rate of speed and inertia. If you momentarily set your shoulders, stop the motion of your hip, and deepen your seat, it will cause the horse to hesitate briefly, blocking the forward motion. The block of your upper body holds your hands in place, while your deepened seat and leg pressure send the horse forward into the block. This action causes the horse to step farther under with his hind feet, which lightens the horse's forehand and rebalances him.

The horse can also be sent forward in a similar manner. If you suddenly sit deep and forward in the saddle, this motion will propel the horse forward.

Your seat can also be used to enhance your leg aid when used for bending or lateral movements, by deepening and adding pressure to one side of the saddle. To use your seat as an inside aid, tip your inside hip down into the saddle and stretch your inside leg long. You must be sitting in the center of the saddle and the center of the horse's back. Be careful to keep your shoulders level and directly above your hip. Your shoulders also must be centered above (not in front of) the hip to be effective as an aid (Fig. 3).

Keep in mind your seat will not be effective if you don't have all your weight on it. Do not tighten your knees and thighs or stand on your irons; that will lighten your seat.

WAIST

Your waist is a shock absorber, which absorbs the bounce of the horse and allows your seat to remain on the saddle. Your waist area must remain relaxed so it can deflect the horse's bounce from going up to your shoulders, causing your arms and hands to bounce and move. In this same area are your stomach muscles. They

35

are used to hold your chest up and keep your upper body from tipping forward. It is important to keep your stomach muscles firm in all down transitions. This will give you extra control of your shoulders. Your stomach muscles are the real strength of your back.

HANDS

Your hands communicate with the horse through the reins. Communication can only take place with contact between your hand and the bit through the reins. Contact is the pressure you hold on the bit with the reins. Correct contact or feel of the bit (amount of pressure or weight), is a very complicated and difficult skill, because it requires a great deal of concentration and sensitivity. Contact that is inadequate, excessive, or inconsistent is one of the leading mistakes in dressage.

For correct contact the first thing to achieve is relaxed arms and hands. Your arms and hands are like an electrical cord connecting you to the horse through the reins. If your arms and hands are tense, it is like creating static and sending it to the horse's mouth. Intermittently losing contact or not maintaining a consistent pressure on the bit is like unplugging and then plugging in an electrical cord. When you do not have contact, you are not talking to the horse.

Your reins should be held with a soft hold rather than a hard hold. A soft hold is achieved by having flexible fingers that squeeze or vibrate the reins. This slight motion massages the bit on the horse's bars and tongue, finessing him into submission. The slight movement of your fingers will also help you to relax your hands. A hard hold (dead or clenched hand equals tension) will only force the horse into submission. Would you rather be finessed or forced into doing something?

Relaxing your hand will help keep it steady. A steady hand is crucial for a steady head on the horse. If you move your hands around or allow the horse to move your hands, the horse will never learn where to carry his head. If you tip your shoulders forward or back, your hands will do the same, causing a loss of consistent contact.

Your arms, hands, and shoulders are relaxed. Your still shoulders are keeping your hands quiet, but your job is not done. There is much more to do. Horses move in a rhythm and your hands must follow. At the walk and canter the horse nods his head as he moves. Your hands must follow the rhythmic motion of the horse in order to keep consistent contact. This following action is accomplished by moving your elbows forward and back to and from your body. Improving your balance and relaxation will enable you to follow the rhythm of the horse with your hands. When the horse bends and curves his body, the outside hand must move forward following the rein and the inside hand must move back following the rein.

Once you have relaxation, and a steady hand that can maintain a consistent contact, you are ready to "talk" to the horse. Contrary to the way most people ride horses, your hands do not stop or turn the horse. All your aids should work harmoniously together to stop or turn the horse. About 90% of riders use too much hand. Your hands are blocking and steadying aids.

Horses are ridden on diagonal aids, inside leg pressure moving the horse to the outside rein. The job of the outside rein is to contain the energy generated by the inside leg. When you squeeze with your legs, it causes the horse to step further under behind. This creates energy which the horse can use to go forward, laterally (sideways), or up (collection or engagement). If you hold consistent firm contact, the horse will step up and into the contact thus becoming engaged. If your hands are not steady and consistent, the energy can escape and not do the job for which your legs are asking; all this energy will go out the front door. This energy must be held to create engagement and suspension.

The consistent contact of the outside rein balances and helps turn the horse. Horses are taught to move away from pressure. When the horse is correctly bent in preparation for a circle or turn, the outside rein contact will help him move into the turn and become an outside boundary.

Remember that all your aids work in combination with one another. The inside rein is probably the most abused aid. Most people attempt to turn the horse with the inside rein, which is a severe error. The job of the inside rein is to relax the horse's jaw through softening (squeezing your fingers, not moving your hand). Through softening, encourage the horse to flex slightly at the throat-latch and neck, which is the start of bending and submission. The work of the inside rein is the preparation for turning -- only the preparation. Generally there should be slightly more contact on the outside rein than the inside during a circle or turn; equal pressure should be held on the reins when moving straight.

Half-halts can be used on the inside or outside rein, or both. If a horse is hanging on a rein, he should be softened or half-halted off. Do not become the horse's fifth leg. He should move on his own four legs in self-carriage. The horse can only hang or pull on you when there is solid contact. To get the horse to release his pull, you must release contact. The horse cannot pull on something that isn't there. The release of contact can be varied from a quick motion of your fingers to dropping contact for several minutes. Softening is a form of contact release. A half-halt is a form of balance adjustment (from forehand to haunches) which can be followed by a release of contact. Momentarily dropping contact on the inside rein will help a horse seek contact on the outside rein. Momentarily dropping contact on both reins will help convince the horse he should try to carry himself, and not count on you to "hold" him up. Be careful to always have leg and seat pressure sending the horse forward.

To make your hands effective, it is also important to check the length of the reins. Too short of rein can restrict the horse's motion and not allow him to stretch through his neck. The reins should be long enough to allow the horse to stretch into his natural neck length, but not so long as to make it difficult to get the horse onto the bit and engage his hind quarters. Your elbows must stay in place; the length of the rein changes. The horse will typically take a longer rein for the walk than for the trot or the canter. Determine the proper length for each gait and keep it. The reins are extensions of your hands, and should be considered as part of a single unit comprising your arms, hands, and reins which work in harmony. Above all, remember your hands must finesse the horse, not force him.

LEGS

Your legs are the navigation center for maneuvering

the horse. The effectiveness of your legs depends upon what part of the horse to which you apply them and the type and consistency of pressure you exert. Remember that your legs (upper calf to inside heel) must be in the proper position under your hip and knees, with your feet parallel to the horse's side. Also, keep in mind, at lower levels the spur is not an aid.

The length of your leg in comparison to the size and shape of the barrel on the horse will also determine your effectiveness. If you have either of the following situations, your aids will be compromised: 1. Long legs on a short girth, round barrel horse. 2. Short legs on a deep girth horse. To deal with either problem, emphasize your aids during corrections, make sure the horse "respects" your leg, and will respond to a light aid. The reason the above situations are difficult is that there are specific areas of the horse where your legs should be used as an aid.

Figure 4 (Pg. 44) shows boxes drawn on the horse's side. These "boxes" are about four inches square. The first box (bend) is right behind the girth. Pressure in this box will bend the horse in the center of his body where he should bend. If you look at the horse's body, you see only three places where the horse can easily curve his spine: at the neck (obviously quite easily, which can be a fault if over bent), at the girth, and at the flank.

Pressure in the bend box will also send his energy forward onto the outside rein. The bend box is only an inside aid. When using your inside leg in the bend box, you will be effective only if your outside leg is farther back in a "turn box." You cannot push the horse's ribs out and offset them, if your outside leg is lying on the same area as the inside leg. The horse will only speed up.

Next is the "go box." Generally both of your legs will be in the go box (inside and outside) to send the horse forward in a straight line. Think of the go boxes as a gas pedal for the horse, creating energy, and sending the horse forward. Pressure in the go boxes also causes the horse to step farther under his body, improving his balance, and enabling him to lighten his forehand. The horse does not raise his forehand to remedy "heavy on the forehand"; he lowers his haunches by stepping further underneath. Horses can pull with the front feet as well as push with the hind feet. A horse pulling in front has more of a tendency to be on the forehand. Engaging the horse's hind quarters lessens the pull from the front feet.

The go box is used for down transitions as well as for going forward. Pressure in the go boxes is especially important in down transitions to keep the horse from falling on his forehand. You are also better able to maintain your balance by using leg pressure, and can keep the horse going forward in the down transition. If the horse loses impulsion during the down transition, he will be more likely to fall on his forehand.

Next are the "turn boxes." The first one is for large circles or turns and the one further back is for small circles or turns. If you are bending the horse, your outside leg should be in one of these boxes. Turn boxes are only on the outside of the horse's body. The top view (Fig. 5, Pg. 45) shows leg positions for a straight or bending frame. As you ride, try to periodically monitor your leg position to be sure you are correct. Sometimes you may need the assistance of a ground person, because what you feel may differ from what is actually happening.

The next aspect of your leg aid is the type and the consistency of the pressure you exert. Ultimately your goal is to get the horse to respond to a very light aid. It is preferable to have the horse sweat more than you. I like to use the squeeze, tap, and then kick hard method. You want an immediate response to your aid. If you don't get one, your aid was not effective. Be sure to let the horse know ignoring you is not appropriate. If the horse does not respond, reorganize the horse right away and repeat your aid with the squeeze, tap, kick method until you get the response you want. Hopefully, the next time you tap the horse, he will respond. When you use a strong leg aid on the horse, be sure to let him go forward with the new energy you asked for.

The type of pressure you apply for an aid will vary with each gait. Generally, the faster you want to go or the more difficult the movement (halt to canter), the pressure you apply will increase. Your inside leg pressure usually squeezes or taps in rhythm with the horse's movement. Your outside leg generally applies a consistent pressure.

HELPFUL REMINDERS

1. Try to keep the horse relaxed, and eliminate tension in your body.

2. Keep your horse's attention.

3. Be sure your aids are applied in the correct area on the horse.

4. Learn the proper use of each aid and the effect it should have on the horse.

5. Use the repeat or reward/punish method to ensure the horse understands the movement.

6. Become part of the horse and work at his physical and mental capacity.

7. Check the frame of the horse. Is he stretching and moving forward?

LEG AIDS

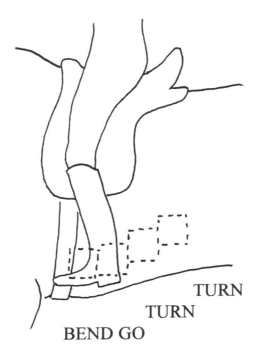

TURN

TURN

BEND GO

Each box on the horse is approximately four inches square. The position of these boxes will vary somewhat depending on the shape of the horse and the length of your leg. The "bend" box is used by your inside leg for bending the horse. The "go" boxes are on both sides of the horse and are used to send the horse forward, to do down transitions, and to halt. The first "turn" box is used by your outside leg to hold the horse's haunches while bending on large circles or turns. The second "turn" box is used by your outside leg to hold the horse's haunches while bending on small circles or turns. Your outside leg will also move to the turn boxes for various transitions and lateral movements.

Figure 4

RIDER AIDS FOR A
STRAIGHT OR BENDING HORSE

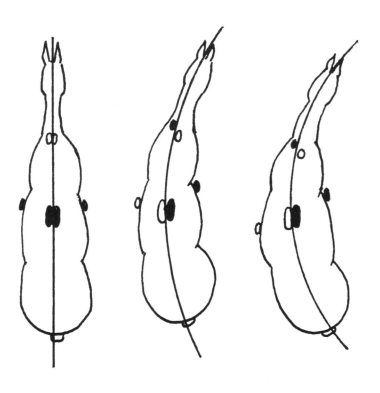

| STRAIGHT LINE | 20M CIRCLE | 10M CIRCLE |
| GO AND STOP | OR TURN | OR TURN |

The dark spots on the horses are the active aids where you will apply more pressure with your hands, legs, and seat. Look at these figures and visualize how you will sit on the horse and how your body will feel.

Figure 5

SHOULDER/SEAT

1. Always keep your shoulders above your hips, and stay centered over the horse.
2. Use your shoulders (not elbows and forearms) to hold your hands.
3. Use stomach muscles to hold up your chest.
4. Think of your waist as a shock absorber.
5. Use your seat as a blocking aid for half-halts and down transitions by momentarily stopping your hip motion.
6. Send the horse forward by deepening your seat and pushing forward in the saddle.
7. Enhance your leg aid by deepening your seat on one side of the saddle.
8. Do not tighten your knees and thighs as this will lighten your seat.

HANDS

1. Maintain consistent, elastic contact with relaxed arms and hands.
2. Hold your hands in place with your shoulders.
3. Follow the horse's motion with your hands at the walk and canter.
4. Do not stop or turn the horse with your hands alone; coordinate all your aids.
5. Block and steady the horse with the outside rein, which helps to balance and turn the horse.
6. Soften with the inside rein to gain submission and encourage (not force) the horse to flex his neck.

7. Be consistent with the length of your rein for each gait.

LEGS

1. Ride with your heels directly below your hip and knees, with your feet parallel to the horse's side.
2. Use your lower leg to send the horse forward and step farther under with his hind legs.
3. Determine where the bend, go, and turn boxes are and try to use them consistently.
4. Make the horse respond to a light aid. Use the squeeze, tap and then kick hard method.
5. Use your inside leg pressure to squeeze or tap in rhythm with the horse, while your outside leg applies consistent pressure.
6. Always have more pressure and activity with your legs than hands.

4. HORSE PSYCHOLOGY

No horse will perform properly and to the best of his ability, unless he is a willing participant in your (not his) endeavor. His first choice would be eating in the pasture. To keep the horse a happy and harmonious partner, the following are certain things you must realize and accept.

1. What is the horse's intelligence level and how does he learn?
2. What type of an animal is he and how much does instinct affect him?
3. How is he affected by the rider?

On the intelligence scale of all animals, the horse is quite low, maybe because of his limited reasoning power and his poor eyesight. Presumably, the rider is much more intelligent than the horse, but you must ride and teach the horse on his level. Also, give the horse some consideration for the length of his attention span, boredom, and mental and physical capabilities. Horses learn best by repetition and reward/punishment methods.

When using repetition to teach the horse a movement, ask for it over and over until he understands. Be sure to be very consistent with your aids in how you ask for a movement. Sometimes asking the horse for a movement in the same spot in the arena will help. Horses are very consistent, repetitive-behavior animals, so use this to your advantage. When trying to teach the horse something, always start with the simplest form of a movement. If you are teaching leg yield, don't start with the trot; start with the walk, then progress to the trot. If at any time you have a problem, go back to an easier gait or movement to help eliminate the resistance. One step back will take you two steps forward. One of the best ways to teach the horse right from wrong is to immediately stop an incorrect movement, reorganize, and start again. Repeat the process until the horse decides to cooperate.

When you have a problem with the horse, discipline him consistently. If you move around too much or change aids during your discipline, the horse will be confused. Stay in position and keep your aid pressure in place. Wait for the horse to mold himself into your aids. When the horse responds correctly reward him, which is the next step in his learning method.

The other part of the horse's learning process is reward/punish. Keep in mind that you are the one desiring perfection. The horse is only doing what he thinks he has to. However, I find some horses do seem to take pleasure in certain movements like medium trot and flying changes.

If the horse does something correctly, praise him with an encouraging tone of voice and body posture -- such as relaxation of your body, a pat on the neck, and maybe a stretch for the horse. If the horse does something wrong, be sure to tell him or he will have no reason to stop doing it wrong. You can use your voice, a slap of your hand, spur, or whip. Measure the type and amount of punishment with the disobedience, keep your emotions in check, and always try to maintain relaxation. Horses are very capable of getting mad. If the horse gets mad or tense, the progress is at a dead end until you do something to get relaxation back.

Another way to discipline the horse without ever getting on him is to improve his ground manners. If he pushes you around and does not obey commands on the ground, the same behavior will come through when you are riding him. Teach the horse to stay in his space and not get in yours. You can also teach the horse to move away from pressure on the ground, and start the movements turn on the forehand, turn on the haunches, and leg yield. This work will teach the horse discipline, and will transfer to your aids when asking the horse for these movements while riding.

Horses can be creative and deliberately resist your aids to avoid the movement you are asking for. Since horses are consistent repetitive animals, he will probably exhibit the same resistance over and over. Learn to anticipate the resistance the horse will make. Determine the proper correction for the resistance and make the correction just before the horse attempts the resistance. If you accomplish the correction and prevent the horse from resisting enough times, the horse will give up and obey your aids correctly.

Imagine a chalk board with two columns -- one for you and one for the horse. Every time the horse gets away with a resistance, he gets two marks on his side. When you make the correction before he can resist, you only get one mark on your side. To make the horse stop resisting, there must be more marks on your side than the horse's side.

The horse of today evolved from an animal in prehistoric times. He is a herd animal that was hunted by predators. Although domesticated, the horse will exhibit defensive measures such as biting, kicking, striking, and running away. The horse's herd instincts remain strong. He wants familiar surroundings, and the company of other horses. Horses exhibit what I call the "cougar syndrome." In a herd one horse watches for the attacking cougar. The others watch this horse and when he runs, they all go. If you are afraid of an object or think the horse will be, he can become frightened or tense because of you. He will shy away from or won't go near objects he doesn't like or understand. These are all survival instincts.

The horse also responds to your emotions. He knows if you are afraid of him or confident, and will take advantage or respect you accordingly. Many well-trained horses will only perform to the level of expertise they perceive you to have. They believe you cannot get them to do more, so they won't do more than they have to. They quickly learn to assess your abilities. (See RELAXATION for the solutions to many of these problems.)

1. Train the horse using the repetition and reward/punishment methods.

2. Be very consistent in the use of aids and in all aspects of working with the horse.

3. Keep things simple and don't overload the horse; he can only absorb so much.

4. Teach good ground manners to improve the horse's performance when he's being ridden.

5. Do not under estimate the herd and survival instincts of the horse.

6. Monitor your emotions because the horse will respond to them.

5. TIME TO START GOING SOMEWHERE

Now that you understand the horse's psyche, you are balanced, in position, have effective aids, and the horse is relaxed, forward, and submissive; it's time to start going somewhere.

Your communication will be greatly enhanced and a lot of resistance will be eliminated, if the information in the following two paragraphs is kept in mind when riding the horse.

Every transition, movement, or exercise you ask of the horse should always have a well planned consistent preparation and execution. The preparation will alert the horse to a new movement. The horse must be taught not to anticipate, but wait for the final aids that tell him to start a new movement. If the horse anticipates a movement, stop, and start again until he learns to wait for your final (execution) aids.

The dressage horse's choices for movement are Forward, Lateral (sideways), and Up (collection); and are always in this order because of difficulty. If the horse is prevented from going forward by hard hands, too short of neck, tension or resistance, he must go somewhere with his energy and will choose lateral. If you wish the horse to move laterally, you must block forward by taking more rein contact or half-halt as you ask for the movement. For up (collection) movements, forward and lateral motion must be blocked with rein contact, half-halts, or leg aids.

When riding the horse you are doing one of three basic things:
1. Riding on a straight line.
2. Riding on a curved line.
3. Changing from one gait to another.

Let's start with the straight line (Fig. 6). It's not as easy as you think, but it will be easier if you look where you want to go. Check your position to be sure you are centered on the horse, have an even rein length, and have equal pressure from your hand, leg, and seat aids.

Some influences that have nothing to do with your aids may alter your line. Horses are prone to fade toward their barn, the in-gate of an arena, or other horses. To compensate for the horse going off track, be sure to use your legs to guide him. If you try to steer with your hands, it will make matters worse. Remember that your hands are the brakes, and your legs the gas pedal. The horse must be going forward from your leg and seat aids with impulsion to go straight. The slow or lazy horse will tend to wander and is better able to evade your aids.

He also will not go straight if there is resistance in the jaw, even if he feels forward. If the horse's jaw feels stiff or locked in place, the horse is resistant. Resistance in the jaw will cause the horse to move his shoulder or hip sideways, because he cannot go freely forward and must go somewhere. He must also want to go where you are sending him. Getting the horse to go straight up the center line toward the judge's box may be difficult if he is afraid of the box. Rather than punishing him with your aids, it would be better to spend some time trying to desensitize him to strange objects.

1. Look straight ahead to where you want to go.
2. Ensure you have even reins, and equal pressure from your hand, leg, and seat aids.

3. Send the horse forward from your leg aids with impulsion to go straight.

4. Keep in mind the horse's herd instincts that can cause him to fade toward his barn or other horses.

5. Eliminate resistance in the horse's jaw which will cause him to weave.

6. Establish confidence in the horse so he will want to go where you are sending him.

STRAIGHT FRAME

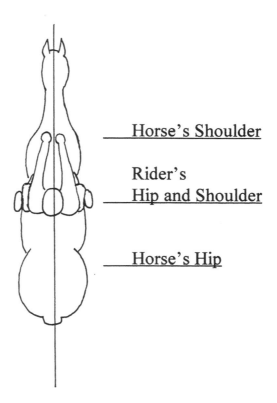

Horse's Shoulder

Rider's
Hip and Shoulder

Horse's Hip

The horse and rider are both going straight forward. The rider's hands, hips, and shoulders are straight across and parallel to the horse.

Figure 6

Riding a curved line such as a circle is also difficult. The reason circles are put in a dressage test is not to see if a rider knows what a circle is. It is to see if a rider can keep the horse on the aids correctly and consistently, to produce a round circle. The horse is ridden on a circle with pressure from your inside leg to the outside rein; which, if used in combination with your outside leg, will keep the horse on track.

It is at this point we are going to talk about bending. The horse can turn in two methods; one is similar to how a motorcycle turns by leaning over to one side. This method strains his body, and especially his legs. It also increases the risk of a fall. The second method, which is the most efficient and safest, is for the horse to curve his spine from ear to tail and match the shape of the circle (Fig. 7, Pg. 62).

To achieve a bend in the horse, apply your aids as follows, starting from your head down to your feet. Turn your head and shoulders as one unit, as though you are wearing a whiplash collar. Most important, look where you want to go and try to envision the track you will ride in the arena footing. Keep your shoulders level. The tendency is to lower your inside shoulder and lean in the direction of the turn, which is incorrect. Keep your hip centered in the saddle, but put more weight on your inside seat bone by stretching your inside leg down. Let your hands follow the turn of your shoulders as the inside hand softens (squeezing, not pulling), the inside rein to encourage the horse to yield and curve his neck. Your inside hand moves closer to you as your outside hand moves farther away and maintains a consistent contact.

Your inside leg hangs at the girth in the bend box, and pushes the horse onto the outside rein. Your inside leg actually bends the horse by displacing his ribs sideways. There are only three places where the horse can easily curve his spine -- the neck, the girth, and the flank. Your inside leg asks for a bend at the girth.

The last part of the bend, the flank, is obtained by using your outside leg. To complete the bend, move your outside leg back to one of the turn boxes and hold a consistent pressure. This will keep the horse from swinging his haunches out to avoid bending (Fig.8, Pg. 63). The outside leg also sends the horse forward around the circle or turn. Failure to use or ineffectiveness of the outside leg aid is a common fault of riders circling or turning horses.

Making a good circle requires a very good preparation and execution. The preparation aspect of circling is:

1. Turning your head and shoulders to look where you are going, and deepening your inside seat bone.
2. Softening the inside rein to encourage neck flexion.
3. Using pressure from your inside leg to move the horse onto the outside rein and create a bend.

The horse should stay on a straight track and not start turning through this point. He is held there by your inside leg and the outside rein. The horse should be bending his body now. The execution part of the circle is sliding your outside leg back to a turn box and applying enough pressure to move the horse off the straight track onto a curved one.

Match the horse's bend in his body to the circle or turn you desire. To help you match the horse's bend to the shape of the circle or turn to be ridden, try to envision a chalk line on the arena footing. The horse has a line along his spine from ears to tail. Match the horse's "spine line" to the chalk line and use your hand and leg aids to maintain the bend.

To change the size of the circle or maintain a correct shape, think of your aids as walls. Move your walls to keep the horse on the track you desire. Remember horses should be taught to move away from pressure. The outside wall consists of the outside rein and your outside leg. The inside wall is your inside leg (not rein). The inside rein can only be used as an inside wall if you cross it over the withers to aid the horse that is falling in on his shoulder. Great care must be taken with the inside rein aid. It can be a disaster if used incorrectly.

If you want to make a circle smaller or maintain a small circle, create more bend by increasing your outside hand and leg aids, which is like closing in the outside wall. Be sure to continue to soften the inside rein and bend the horse around your inside leg. Never pull on the inside rein to make a smaller circle or turn the horse.

To make a larger circle, relax the outside rein and leg aids and increase pressure on your inside leg. Do not attempt to enlarge your circle or move the horse laterally by pulling on the outside rein. If you tip the horse's head to the outside, he will fall in on his shoulder and actually make the circle smaller or move the opposite direction you want. When a horse is being resistant, his shoulder will generally move the opposite direction his head is pointed.

Be sure you send the horse forward onto the circle. Horses moving forward with impulsion stay on track better. Ride the horse like you would drive a sports car, and accelerate into the turns. Your hands are the brakes and your legs are the gas pedals. When you ask the horse to submit to the inside rein and move onto the outside rein, this action can slow him down. You must add enough leg aid to counter this resistance.

The next step in bending is to change from one bend to another. You can start with changes across a diagonal, then change in a figure eight, and finally, change in a serpentine. Changing bend is commonly called change of rein, because your inside leg pushes the horse onto the other (new outside) rein. A lot more happens in this process.

Before starting a change of bend, have a plan and know where you want to go. The process for changing bend is the same as preparing to ride a circle. Begin with your head and shoulders turning in the new direction. Look where you want to go, soften the new inside rein, and weight your inside seat bone as your inside leg comes against the horse at the girth. This is where the change of rein occurs. As you soften the new inside rein, hold the new outside rein firm and steady. Your inside leg pushes the horse onto the new outside rein and curves his body to match the curve of your next movement. Don't forget to apply your outside leg in a turn box to complete the change of bend.

Your change of bend will be enhanced and you can help the horse maintain his balance, if you half-halt prior to the change. Also, be sure to send the horse forward into the new bend. Constant aid adjustments are required to maintain the bend. Be ready for the resistance and try to make the correction as fast as the horse resists (remember the chalk board from Horse Psychology).

When bending the horse or riding a circle/turn, four things can happen. Hopefully, the horse will bend correctly and be consistent, but he could fall in on his shoulder, fade out through his outside shoulder, flip his haunches out, or increase the tempo.

If the horse falls in on his shoulder, apply more inside leg and push him back onto the outside rein (Fig. 8). Be sure there is more contact on the outside rein than on the inside rein. The inside rein does not turn the horse. If over used, the inside rein can cause the horse to fall in on his shoulder. Generally when the horse falls in, he counter flexes (bends the wrong way). Use your inside leg to keep the horse from changing the bend and counter flexing. Check to be sure the horse is bent to match the curve you want prior to starting a circle or turn. The inside rein can be crossed over the withers to aid your inside leg, but great care must be taken to not over use this aid, or the horse will lie on it.

If the horse is fading out through his outside shoulder, tighten the outside rein and apply your outside leg to bring the horse in (Fig. 8). Once again the inside rein will not help keep the horse from fading out, because it can cause the horse to over bend in his neck. If there is more bend in the horse's neck than his back, the horse will fade out through his outside shoulder.

If the horse is flipping his haunches out while circling or turning, increase your outside leg aid (Fig. 7). Your leg may not be back far enough or may not be effective. An outside leg takes a lot of strength and balance.

If the horse increases his tempo instead of bending when you put your inside leg on, a little more contact on the outside rein will control the speed and make the horse bend. Remember the horse's three choices of motion: forward, lateral, or up, in that order.

1. Look ahead, check your position, and try to envision the circle.
2. Prepare well for bending before starting the circle or turn.
3. Ride from your inside leg to the outside rein, creating a bend.
4. Do not turn the horse with the inside rein.
5. Obtain a correct bend from ear to tail.
6. Make sure your legs are in the bend and turn boxes and accelerate slightly.
7. Adjust the shape of the circle by moving the horse laterally with your inside or outside leg, and the outside rein.

BENDING FRAME

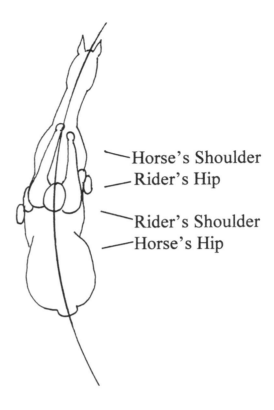

Horse's Shoulder
Rider's Hip

Rider's Shoulder
Horse's Hip

The horse and rider are in the correct frame and position for a circle or turn. Note the position of the rider's hands, legs, and shoulders and how they fit the curve of the horse's body. Both the horse's and rider's hips are parallel; as are the horse's and rider's shoulders.

Figure 7

62

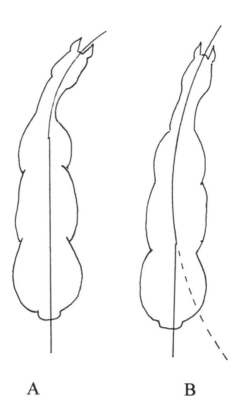

A   B

HORSE A: This horse is over bent in the neck. Generally this horse will not bend in the body. The horse with this incorrect frame usually will fade out at the shoulder. This is a bad fault which is caused by pulling on the inside rein instead of riding from the inside leg to the outside rein.

HORSE B: This horse is swinging his haunches out. This fault is not as severe as figure A. The horse is usually not stepping under with his inside hind leg. Generally this fault is caused by an ineffective outside leg.

Figure 8

UP TRANSITIONS

Transitions from one gait to another are called "up" and "down." Up transitions increase momentum and down transitions decrease momentum. Let's start with up transitions such as halt to walk, walk to trot, and trot to canter. Remember a horse's choices of motion: forward, lateral, and up. Depending on the amount of collection you desire in the new gait, you will have to adjust your aids to compensate for the above three choices. Basically, the more collection you desire or the greater change of gait (halt to canter), the more you will emphasize your aids. Also, you need a good preparation. No matter how well you execute a transition, it will not be done well unless the horse is moving correctly in the current gait, before changing to another. If the horse is above the bit in the trot and you make an up transition, he will be above the bit in the canter.

The transition for halt to walk or trot, and walk to trot, are the same except for the amount of pressure applied with your hand, leg, and seat aids. The goal for up transitions is to have the horse move forward with impulsion in a straight line without resistance. The horse should not pull on your hand or come above the bit. In the case of up transitions, the horse should step underneath with his hind feet and push himself forward.

To achieve an up transition, start with your aids from your head to your feet. To start, lift your chin and use your eyes to look up where you want to go. Raise your chest and be sure your back and stomach muscles are ready to hold your shoulders in place, in case the horse pulls on your hand. Be careful not to lean forward or let the horse pull you out of position. That will put him on his forehand and enable him to pull with his front feet rather than push with his haunches as he should. Your shoulders coming forward, also causes a loss of contact in the reins and allows the horse to come above the bit. Release tension in your arms and hands, but do not release contact.

To keep the horse from coming above the bit in the up transition, which is the most common fault, contact must be maintained. Use your shoulders not elbows or forearms to maintain contact, while your fingers soften through the reins, giving a soft not hard hold. Most horses will raise their poll and shorten their neck slightly as they correctly make an up transition. Therefore, as you increase tempo, the reins should be shorter, especially from halt to trot.

The up transition preparation involving the reins starts by stretching your hands forward, opening your elbow angle, and inching your fingers up the reins to achieve the desired rein length for the next gait. The distance from the bit to your shoulder must remain the same until the horse moves into another gait. If the bit to shoulder distance changes, his tempo or frame may change, and it should not. As the horse moves off into the new gait, bring your hands back to their proper position, maintaining contact. Deepen your seat and set your hip forward in the saddle.

The last aid to be applied for the up transition is your leg. Remember, if you are going in a straight line, have your legs in the go boxes. For a curved line, have your legs in the bend and turn boxes (Fig. 4). Stretch your legs down, being careful not to overbend your knees and pull them up as you apply pressure. Try to make your upper body wait for the horse to go. Only your legs and

65

deepening seat should send the horse forward. The weight of your upper body along with your back and seat are driving aids, so your shoulders must stay directly above your hip. If your shoulders come forward, you are driving the horse backward and hindering his forehand.

For the transition up to canter, be sure the horse is on the outside rein with some softening on the inside rein. It is especially important to keep your shoulders back with your chest stretched up and that you wait -- wait for the transition. Do not "help" the horse depart by tipping your shoulders forward; instead, deepen your inside seat, and offset your legs in the bend and turn boxes. Your inside leg applies pressure and sends the horse forward onto the outside rein. Your inside leg also helps the horse's inside hind leg come forward to get the correct lead.

1. Look up and where you want to go. Do not look at the horse's head.
2. Make a clear, consistent preparation.
3. Keep your shoulders above your hip and don't lean forward.
4. Shorten your reins to the proper length for the next gait before departing.
5. Maintain a firm but soft contact through the reins.
6. Use your shoulders, not elbows and forearms, to hold your hands in place.
7. Send the horse forward with your legs and seat.
8. Wait for the horse to go; don't get ahead of him.

Down transitions are rather difficult and require a lot of careful preparation. The horse must continue moving forward and not fall on his forehand. Very little pressure on the reins is necessary for a down transition. Do not pull on the reins. There is a big difference between pulling and holding. Holding your hands in place with your shoulders is correct. Pulling back on the reins is never correct. Your change of body motion and rhythm along with leg pressure, and a deepening seat are the keys to down transitions.

For preparation into the down transition, once again stretch your chest up and use your stomach and back muscles to hold your shoulders so you don't tip forward. As the horse makes a transition down, he has a decrease in momentum and inertia. You must prepare to match the change in momentum by keeping your shoulders directly above your hip. Your shoulders coming forward causes you to lose contact and an effective seat aid. Your hands held by your shoulders must stay in place to maintain contact.

For a down transition the horse is ridden forward from your leg and seat aids into contact. Without contact the horse will lose balance and then increase tempo trying to regain his balance. Be careful not to let the horse hang on your hand or you could end up with the same problem.

Half-halt to ensure the horse is in self-carriage prior to the down transition and soften with your fingers throughout the transition. Block or stop your body motion and rhythm (mostly hip) as an aid to bring the horse down. The pressure of your leg and deepening seat will help the horse step under behind, enabling him to keep his forehand elevated.

For an effective aid, make sure your legs don't slip forward. They should be directly under your hip in the go boxes, which will also help you maintain your balance. Your leg will then be in place to ensure the horse continues going forward.

The horse will require a longer rein as you decrease tempo in down transitions, especially to the walk. As the horse completes the down transition, be sure to slip the reins out to the proper length for the new gait.

1. Prepare very carefully for this difficult transition.
2. Do not use your hand to pull the horse into a down transition.
3. Maintain a soft but firm contact on the reins.
4. Keep your shoulders slightly behind your hip, using strong stomach muscles.
5. Use your shoulders, not elbows and forearms, to hold your hands in place.
6. Half-halt prior to the down transition.
7. Use a block/stop of your body motion and rhythm (mostly hip) as an aid.
8. Deepen your seat with all your weight in the saddle, not in the irons.
9. Be sure to ride the horse forward with your lower legs under your hip in the "go boxes."
10. Slip the reins to the correct rein length for the new gait.
11. Go back to an easier transition, if you have problems.

Transitions into and out of the halt are about the most difficult. When riding the horse in a dressage test, you have to halt twice on a centerline; and depending on the test, at A or C.

For the transition from the halt to trot, the horse must be submissive to your hand. If the horse resists by stiffening or pulling, he will raise his poll and come above the bit. To prevent this and keep the horse on the bit, start with your position. Review strength advantage through proper position (Fig. 3).

Raise your chin and look straight ahead, not at the horse's head. Your goal is to ride a straight line, so you need to look for that line to get it. Lift your chest and set your shoulders above your hip. Make sure your stomach muscles and back are ready to hold your shoulders in place. Your arms and hands should be extended slightly forward, so the horse can have the length of neck he needs at the halt, and the reins will be the correct length when the horse trots. Your seat should be deep and have all your weight shifting to the front of the saddle. Your lower legs move back to the go boxes (Fig. 4), sending the horse forward into steady contact held by your shoulders.

Do not let the horse pull your hands or shoulders forward. If you feel resistance, soften with your fingers, but keep your hands in place and maintain contact. If the horse feels a loss of contact or slack in the rein, he will try to escape through it and come above the bit.

Be careful not to hold the horse too hard onto the bit at the halt. Remember that the horse's choice of movement is forward, lateral, and up. If the horse is prevented from going forward by the stiffness of a hard hold or by his own resistance to the bit, he will shift his hind quarters or shoulders sideways and go off the centerline. If you are having difficulty with resistance to the bit and coming above the bit in the halt to trot transition, first check your position and then use of aids.

The only parts of your body that send the horse forward are your lower legs and seat. Wait with your upper body for the horse to leave. Be sure your reins are not so long you cannot maintain contact or you will end up with your elbows behind the center of your side. Do not have your reins so short they shorten the horse's neck or encourage you to tip forward.

If you still have problems, you may be asking too much too soon. Try some transitions of walk to trot for a few times and gradually reduce the walk steps.

In the transition from trot to halt you may experience the same resistance encountered in the up transition -- coming above the bit and crookedness. Once again, your position is critical. Review strength advantage through proper position (Fig. 3) and visualize your shoulders slightly behind your hip.

This transition and all down transitions are not accomplished by pulling back on the horse's mouth. The trot to halt transition is created by riding the horse forward to the bit which is held by your shoulders and back. Think of this transition like riding the horse to a wall. Upon reaching a wall the horse willingly halts. The bit, held by your back and shoulders, is the wall.

Use a block/stop of your body motion and rhythm (mostly hip) as an aid for the transition into halt. Your hip must be centered deep in the saddle with relaxed knees and thighs for an effective seat aid. Ride the horse forward from leg and seat aids to consistent firm contact held by your shoulders. Once again prevent the horse from falling on his forehand with a half-halt prior to the transition to establish self-carriage. Keep your lower leg under your hip in the "go boxes" to ensure the horse steps under behind.

To keep the horse in the halt once he stops, take all the tension out of your body and relax. Only use enough leg on the horse to keep him from stepping back.

Keep in mind, horses are repetitive behavior animals. The horse will probably repeat the same resistances in the halt over and over. If the horse halts with his haunches left every time, you will need to make a correction for this every time. When the horse halts crooked, first determine if the haunches or shoulders are off center line. If the haunches are off center line, hold your lower leg against that side of the horse before he halts. If the shoulders are fading out, hold extra contact on that side of the horse before he halts. These corrections will also help crookedness in halt departures.

If you are having problems with halt transitions, make sure you are using your body motion and rhythm correctly. Always use stronger leg than hand aids, and be sure you are not creating excessive tension in your muscles. Be steady and consistent with your aids.

1. Plan ahead and prepare for the transition.

2. Be sure the horse is relaxed and submissive before you ask for a transition into or out of the halt.

3. Raise your chin and look straight ahead.

4. Keep your shoulders above or slightly behind your hip.

5. Do not pull the horse into the halt with your hands; instead maintain a soft but firm contact.

6. Use your shoulders, not elbows and forearms, to hold your hands in place.

7. Do not have your reins so short they shorten the horse's neck or encourage you to tip forward.

8. Be sure your reins are not too long or they will cause you to lose contact or bring your elbows behind the center of your side.

9. Use stronger leg than hand aids and try to eliminate tension in your muscles.

10. Half-halt prior to the transition.

11. Use a block/stop of your body motion and rhythm (mostly hip) as an aid for the halt transition.

12. Ride the horse forward with your lower leg under your hip in the "go boxes."

13. Deepen your seat with all your weight in the saddle, not on the irons.

14. Let the horse take a few walk steps into or out of the halt if you have problems.

6.   STEP BY STEP REVIEW

The preceding chapters have covered five things -- GO, STOP, RIDE A STRAIGHT LINE, RIDE A CURVED LINE, AND CHANGE OF GAIT.   If you consistently follow the step by step instructions in the order given below, the above movements will greatly improve.   When things go wrong and problems develop, first check your position and tension.   Be sure the horse is relaxed and going forward, and you are getting submission.   Always go back to an easier gait or movement to correct a problem.

GO AND UP TRANSITIONS

1. Keep your eyes up and look where you intend to go.
2. Keep your shoulders above your hip with your chest raised.
3.   Extend your hands forward and low keeping the reins even and the correct length for the next gait.
4.   Be sure the rein contact is firm, held by soft squeezing fingers.
5. Hold your hands in place with your shoulders, not your elbows and forearms.
6. Release all the tension in your arms.
7. Deepen your seat and push your hip to the front of the saddle.
8. Slide your lower legs to the go boxes (walk and trot) or the bend and first turn box (canter).
9. Half-halt and then ask for the transition.
10. Wait with your upper body for the horse to leave.

11. Bring your hands back to the normal position as the horse departs.

12. Be sure the horse is moving correctly before the transition if changing gait.

STOP AND DOWN TRANSITIONS

1. Keep your chin up and your chest raised with your shoulders slightly behind your hip.

2. Be sure the rein contact is firm, held by soft, squeezing fingers.

3. Hold your hands in place with your shoulders, not your elbows and forearms. (Never pull the horse into a halt or down transition with your hands.)

4. Deepen your seat in the front of the saddle.

5. Slide your lower legs to the go boxes and under your hip.

6. Do not weight the irons or grip with your knees or thighs.

7. Half-halt and then ask for the transition.

8. Block/Stop your body motion and rhythm (mostly hip) as an aid.

9. Ride forward to firm soft hands held by your shoulders.

STRAIGHT LINES

1. Keep your eyes up and look where you intend to go.

2. Raise your chest and keep your shoulders above your hip.

3. Sit centered in the saddle and also be sure the saddle is centered on the horse.

4. Have your hands low and level with both reins the same length, and with even pressure on the bit.

5. Keep the horse's head directly in front of his shoulders and facing your target.

6. Put both lower legs in the go boxes, sending the horse forward.

7. Use one leg or the other to push the horse sideways and forward to correct crookedness or fading.

8. Never correct crookedness or fading with your hands. The horse will slow down and weave.

9. Try to eliminate any resistance in the horse's jaw.

CURVED LINES

1. Turn your head and shoulders as one unit.

2. Keep your eyes up and look where you intend to go; for a circle try to envision the track ahead.

3. Maintain contact on the outside rein.

4. Soften the inside rein and encourage the horse to flex his neck (don't pull).

5. Never turn the horse with the inside rein.

6. Keep your shoulders level and do not lean in.

7. Deepen your inside seat bone.

8. Prepare for the bend with your inside leg in the bend box while you are still going straight.

9. Start the circle or turn by moving your outside leg back to either turn box and applying pressure.

10. Adjust the shape of your circle with your inside or outside leg and outside rein aids.

7. WHAT IS "ON THE BIT?"

The horse that is on the bit is moving enthusiastically, freely, and naturally forward. He must have the three basic requirements for dressage -- relaxation, desire to go forward, and submission (to both hand and leg). The energy (impulsion) created by your legs and seat causes the horse's hind feet to step well under his body. The energy of his thrust is transmitted up to his hip, across his back to the top of his neck, extends down his forehead over his nose, and ON top of THE BIT (Fig. 9). An added ingredient to this energetic, stretching step is a spring (suspension) in his stride. Some of this energy must be captured and used for the spring. This is where contact comes into play. If you have slack in your reins, the energy will go out the front door and escape. Using your shoulders and a steady, soft hand keeping consistent contact, will contain the energy and help the horse elevate his step.

Think of the horse as a nine foot long object. Compressing the horse between the energy of your legs and seat, and the consistent contact held by your hands and shoulders will make him an eight foot long object, springing higher off the ground and raising his back. If you imagine the horse's spine as a straight line from the ears to tail, the nine foot long horse's "spine-line" is flat. When you properly achieve collection and engagement in the horse, this line becomes curved with a slight rise in the middle. The overall length of the line is still the same, but it has changed shape and now fits in an eight foot long space. Another way to envision the horse on the bit, is that he has stretched out his vertebrae from ears to tail by extending his neck and raising his back. This makes him more elastic and supple. The stretched vertebrae enable you to sit more comfortably and to bend and maneuver the horse. The horse must be relaxed to achieve a proper stretch.

Be careful not to shorten the horse's neck while you are trying to get him on the bit. If his neck is too short, his back will be stiff because his vertebrae are squeezed together. His stride will also be shortened because he will not reach and stretch with his legs. He will also try to lengthen out his neck by coming above the bit. You cannot pull the horse's nose under his ears; his ears must be pushed over his nose by your leg and seat aids. In other words, the horse must be ridden forward onto the bit by your legs and seat.

To determine if the horse is going forward and has impulsion, look at the horse in profile; especially look at the two front legs or the two hind legs. The area from the horse's bottom body line down both front or hind legs to the hoof forms an upside down V (Fig. 9). The wider the V is at the horse's hooves, the bigger the stride. The size of the V for the front legs should match the V of the hind legs. If the horse is tracking up or over, the two Vs will touch or overlap.

To determine if the horse is on the bit when mounted, look at the top line of the horse's neck. If the neck appears flat on top and is ascending from the withers to ears, the horse is above the bit and in front of the vertical (Fig. 12, Pg. 88). There should be a slight upward curve in the middle of the neck's top line (Fig 10, Pg. 82). The area six to seven inches behind the horse's ears must be horizontal and parallel to the ground. If this six to seven inch area is tipped lower at the ears, the horse is behind the vertical. If the horse has come behind the vertical, he is evading the bit. The cause could be an uncomfortable bit or a rider with hard, stiff hands. The correction is to lighten contact and increase leg pressure, to encourage the horse to move forward to the bit. Generally a sharp tap with your leg will persuade the horse to raise his poll. Remember the neck must be stretched long at all times.

Following are some causes of tension that can reduce the horse's desire to move forward onto the bit and decrease flexibility:

1. Resistance to the bit caused by a hard hand or uncomfortable bit.
2. Reins held too short causing a short, tight neck.
3. Stiffness in a rider who is not relaxed or following the horse's motion.
4. Discomfort or confusion that is caused by an unbalanced rider.
5. Confusion caused by improper aids.
6. Pain caused by improperly fitting equipment.
7. Muscle soreness or hoof pain.
8. Fatigue or lack of nutrition.

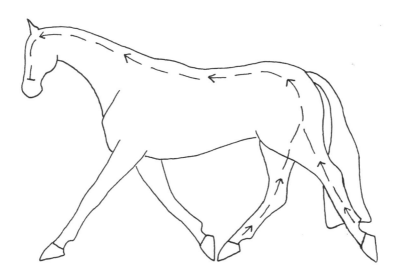

The energy of the horse's hind leg thrust is transmitted up to his hip, across his back to the top of his neck, extends down his forehead over his nose, and ON top of THE BIT.

Figure 9

8.   CORRECT DRESSAGE FRAME

ON THE BIT WITH A CORRECT FRAME

The following figures depict the most common frames seen in lower level dressage horses. Fig. 10 shows the horse we all want; he is ON THE BIT. The following are some of the factors that make him on the bit.

1. Jaw relaxation that allows him to flex at the poll.
2. Neck that is long, stretched, and naturally elevated with a properly curved top line.
3. Forearms and shoulders reaching freely forward.
4. Hind legs stepping well underneath and over the front hoof print.
5. Energy or impulsion of the horse.

To achieve the "on the bit" horse, try to accomplish the following conditions:

1. Be sure the horse is in good health and is getting the proper nutrition he needs for the level of work you expect him to perform.
2. Check your equipment to ensure it fits the horse properly and allows you to maintain a position for effective aids.
3. Keep the horse relaxed and attentive.
4. Do not ride the horse until his is tired, and do not drill him to death. End your workout on a positive note while the horse is still fresh.
5. Monitor your position often to ensure your body parts are in place to apply effective aids.

6. Send the horse forward with an energetic and lively step using your leg and seat aids.

7. Be careful not to rush the horse or he will be unbalanced.

8. Ride in rhythm with the motion of the horse and try to free your body of tension (especially forearms and hands).

9. Apply clear, consistent aids to get and keep the horse on the bit.

10. Keep in mind you must ride the horse onto the bit with your leg. You cannot pull the horse onto the bit with your hands, or you will end up with the horse shown in Fig. 11.

The horse in a correct frame exhibits relaxation, stretching strides, and impulsion.

Figure 10

Fig. 11 shows the horse we think is on the bit because his face is vertical. However, he actually has a severe fault and is being ridden backwards (with more hand than leg). The following are the factors that make him NOT on the bit.

1. The horse is not stretched through his neck.
2. The bulging lower muscle of the neck shows resistance.
3. The horse is not stepping under with his hind legs.
4. The horse's forearms and shoulders are not reaching forward because of the short neck.
5. The shortened stride does not show any impulsion.

The first indication that the horse in Fig. 11 has an incorrect frame is the bulge in the bottom of the neck, which indicates a short, stiff neck caused by resistance. Resistance in the jaw or neck will cause the step of the hind legs to shorten. A short, stiff neck will also block the movement of the shoulders.

The horse can be pushed onto his forehand if his neck is too short, and you are using excessive leg to send him forward. The hind end of the horse will actually "run over" the front end. When horses break stride during a medium walk, this is often the problem. Never attempt to put a horse on the bit by pulling his nose in with your hand.

The lack of stretch in the neck could have several causes: nonacceptance of the bit, improperly fitting saddle, a hard, stiff hand, too short of rein, or lack of an effective leg aid. The corrections for the horse in Fig. 11 are:

1. Check to be sure the bit fits the horse and is suitable. You may need to longe the horse in side reins until he becomes comfortable with the bit.
2. Ensure your saddle fits the horse properly and allows you to maintain a correct position.
3. Monitor your upper body position and try to hold your hands with your shoulders.
4. Relax your hands and be sure there is no tension in your elbows and forearms, because hard, stiff arms are a common cause of the horse depicted Fig. 11.
5. Try to move in a rhythm with the horse.
6. Be sure your reins are long enough to allow the horse to stretch his neck. Your goal is to encourage the horse to stretch forward to the bit by using your legs and seat to create energy.
7. Do not try to get the horse on the bit by pulling his nose in; you must push his ears out over his nose with your leg and seat aids.
8. Always ride the horse with more leg pressure than hand.

The horse in a restricted frame exhibits a tight jaw, shortened up-side-down neck (bulging lower muscle), lack of stretch, and no freedom in the stride.

Figure 11

The horse in Fig. 12 is above the bit and expressing a great deal of resistance. The following are the factors that make him above the bit.

1. The horse no longer has his forehead over his nose in a vertical line.
2. The telltale bulge in the lower neck muscle also shows resistance (up-side-down).
3. The top line of the neck is flat and ascending from the withers to ears.
4. The blocking of energy by resistance has stopped the horse from going through his back.
5. The horse is not stepping under with his hind legs.
6. There is no reaching forward with his forearms and shoulders.
7. The shortened stride does not show any impulsion.

The corrections for the horse in Fig. 12 are:

1. Notice that this horse is lacking two of the basic requirements for dressage -- relaxation and submission.
2. Check your equipment to be sure it fits you and the horse comfortably and properly.
3. Make an assessment of your position, use of aids and body tension; you could be the cause of this problem.
4. Be sure that your reins are the same length, you have a correct length of rein, and you are riding

with a steady, sympathetic hand and elastic fingers.

5. Reestablish relaxation by allowing the horse to stretch his back and neck.

6. Soften the inside or stiff rein to relax the horse's jaw and round the top line of the neck.

7. Send the horse forward with your leg and seat aids into consistent contact, once relaxation and a stretched frame are restored.

8. Go back to the walk to make your correction, if the resistance is at the trot or canter.

9. Go back to an easier movement to establish relaxation and submission, if the resistance is occurring when attempting a difficult movement.

The horse that is above the bit is resistant to the rider's hand or the bit itself. He generally has a shortened neck and stride. The top line of the horse's neck is flat and there is a bulging muscle in the lower neck. The horse's nose is also in front of the vertical line from forehead to nose.

Figure 12

LACK OF IMPULSION

The horse in Fig. 13 is not on the bit, but at least his frame is better, and he is not being as poorly ridden as the horses in Figs. 11 and 12.   This incorrect frame is indicated by the following factors.

1. The horse's biggest fault is lack of impulsion.
2. He also does not have suspension.
3. He is not stepping under with his hind legs or reaching forward with his forearms and shoulders.
4. He does have a nice stretch in his neck, but he is being allowed to fall on his forehand.

The corrections for the horse in Fig. 13 are:

1. Create some energy for impulsion by adding more leg and seat, or make what aids are being used more effective with spurs or a whip to get his attention.
2. Maintain contact with your hands and shoulders to hold the energy created by your leg and seat aids, which will add engagement and suspension to the impulsion.
3. Hold a soft, steady contact without tension in your arms.
4. Half-halt using your leg and seat aids to encourage the horse to step farther under with his hind legs, and help the horse shift his weight from his forehand to his haunches.

LACK OF IMPULSION

The horse with a lack of impulsion exhibits relaxation, but does not have any impulsion (energy). He is not stepping under with his hind legs, which allows him to be heavy on the forehand.

Figure 13

9. MOVEMENTS FOR SUBMISSION AND SUPPLING

The Step By Step Review and the following basic dressage movements are a numerical quick reference. You will notice that each section starts with instructions for your head and moves down to instructions for your feet. Consistency is one of the most important aspects of your dressage aids. Using your aids from head to foot will make it easier for you to remember each step and be consistent.

Every movement should have a good preparation and an execution. Your aids from head to seat are generally part of the preparation, and your lower leg aids are the execution of the movement. Therefore, using your aids from head to foot is not only easy for you, but it is very applicable for the sequence of aids to be used in almost every dressage movement.

Repeat each of the following movements several times using the numerical steps, until the horse accepts and understands your aids. If you are consistent, the horse will be too.

The movements in the following figures are difficult. It will be very helpful to watch experienced riders and horses perform the movements, so you will have a clear picture in your mind. A ground person who can tell you if what you feel is actually happening, or if your movement is correct or incorrect, is also helpful. Riding the following movements in front of mirrors or a video camera will be of assistance.

GROUND WORK

The first thing the horse needs to learn and never forget, is to move away from pressure. Use the palm of your hand to push against several different parts (head, hip, neck, shoulder, etc.) of the horse. He should easily move away. If not, use the same method as you do with your leg when mounted -- push, push harder, then slap him until you get a response and he moves. This is also a safety feature. The horse must respect your space and stay out of it. He should be like a soldier who stands at attention until given a command to move.

Teach the horse some of the same movements you will be doing when mounted, from the ground (turn on the forehand, turn on the haunch, and side pass). These are good movements to use for teaching the horse to move away from pressure. This discipline will be good for establishing your "I am the boss" relationship with the horse. When doing these movements be sure the horse is basically moving forward from your pressure, and is never backing away from you unless asked to.

The horse should also be taught to allow you to turn his head from side to side while standing still or walking. Start by using a carrot to encourage the horse to bring his head around to his side. Gradually eliminate the carrot, and always praise the horse for everything he does correctly.

One aspect to consider in a dressage horse is flexibility. Horses are left and right handed just like people. They will be stiffer to one side than the other. Dressage basically asks the horse to be ambidextrous. Think how hard that would be for you. The above carrot trick works well. Standing on the ground and stretching the horse's legs forward, back, and to the side also helps. Work on the following movements is required to gain equal flexibility on both sides.

After completing your ground work start riding the horse, and teach him to move from your inside leg onto the outside rein. This is your diagonal aid and will be used extensively throughout your dressage career. Diagonal aids help to balance and engage the horse, by sending the energy created by your inside leg to consistent contact held by the outside rein. Almost all movements are performed with diagonal aids. The shoulder-fore movement is very good to teach diagonal aids and is used to begin teaching shoulder-in.

In addition to teaching the horse to move from your inside leg to the outside rein, you must also teach the horse to step under with his inside hind leg. The following movements will help teach the horse to step under with his inside hind leg. These are the building block movements for dressage. Athletic agility, balance, engagement, and suppleness, will all be enhanced through these movements.

SHOULDER-FORE

1. Walk down the long side of the arena.
2. Keep your eyes up, look ahead down the rail, and move your inside shoulder back slightly.
3. Soften the inside rein (don't pull) to encourage the horse to flex his neck and move his head in front of his inside shoulder.
4. Hold contact on the outside rein. (Your goal is to get contact off the inside rein and onto the outside rein.)
5. Keep your hips centered in the saddle and your shoulders level.
6. Deepen your inside seat bone.
7. Use your inside leg in the bend box to keep the horse on the rail.
8. Do not allow the horse to follow his nose in off the rail; he must listen to your inside leg.
9. Lay your outside leg against the horse in the go box to help keep him going forward.
10. Continuously maintain relaxation, stretch, and forward motion.
11. Half-halt periodically to ensure the horse stays in self-carriage.
12. Teach the horse to maintain this frame from your inside leg aid rather than inside rein, by occasionally dropping the inside rein.
13. Use the inside rein only as a reminder.
14. Try this movement at the trot and canter once the horse accepts it at the walk.
15. See Fig. 14.

SHOULDER-FORE

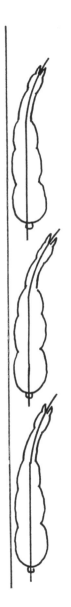

This is an engagement and suppling movement used to teach the horse to move from the inside leg to the outside rein. This movement is also used to begin teaching the horse shoulder-in. Notice how the horse's hips and shoulders stay on the rail, with only the neck bending to the inside.

Figure 14

1. Walk the horse down the center of the arena.
2. Increase the contact on the outside rein and slow the tempo almost to a halt.
3. Move your inside shoulder back slightly.
4. Soften lightly on the inside rein and maintain a slight neck flexion. Do not overuse the inside rein or the horse will spin in his center like a merry-go-round horse.
5. Keep your hip centered in the saddle and your shoulders level.
6. Deepen your inside seat bone.
7. Slide your inside leg back to the last turn box to influence the hind quarters.
8. Push the haunches around making certain the horse is crossing his hind feet one in front of the other, never in back.
9. Keep the horse's front feet stepping up and down in place and slightly forward.
10. Half-halt periodically to ensure the horse stays in self-carriage.
11. Do only a 180-degree turn and immediately walk the horse forward.
12. Maintain relaxation and a stretched frame.
13. See Fig. 15.

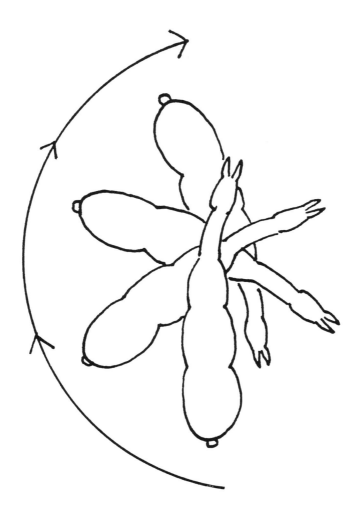

This is a movement where the horse steps sideways, crossing his hind feet one in front of the other, while the front feet move in place and slightly step forward. It is used to teach the horse engagement and suppleness.

Figure 15

LEG YIELD

1. Walk the horse down the quarter line (about fifteen feet away from the rail) of the arena.

2. Establish contact on the outside rein and keep it.

3. Soften the inside rein very lightly, but keep the horse's head centered in front of his shoulders. Do not overuse this rein or the horse will trail his haunches and not stay parallel to the rail.

4. Keep your hips centered in the saddle and your shoulders level and straight.

5. Look where you want to go. Choose an object at the end of an imaginary diagonal line.

6. Slide your inside leg back to the last turn box and push the horse onto the outside rein.

7. Use the outside leg in the go box only to send the horse forward.

8. Coordinate your outside rein and inside leg aids to keep the horse's body parallel to the rail.

9. Use a few turn on the forehand steps to straighten the horse if the haunches start to trail. When the horse is once again parallel to the rail, continue the leg yield.

10. Half-halt periodically to ensure the horse stays in self-carriage.

11. Keep the horse relaxed, stretched and moving forward.

12. Try the movement at sitting trot when the horse does well at the walk.

13. See Fig. 16.

LEG YIELD

This is a movement in which the horse moves forward and sideways at the same time, keeping his body parallel to the rail. The horse should cross both front and hind legs. It is used to teach the horse engagement and suppleness.

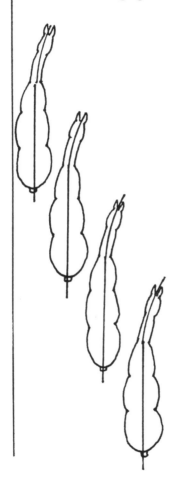

Figure 16

SHOULDER-IN

1. Walk down the long side of the arena, prepare well for the bend appropriate for a 10 M circle and start the circle.
2. Secure the horse on the outside rein with your inside leg during the circle.
3. Start the movement as you reapproach the rail.
4. Let the horse continue on the circle one or two steps beyond the rail and around the circle; and then apply the following aids simultaneously as listed:

    a. lighten your outside leg,
    b. increase contact on the outside rein,
    c. push the horse onto the outside rein with your inside leg.

5. Allow the horse's inside shoulder to come in off the rail the equivalent of one hoof track, as the horse steps in through the bend.
6. Be sure the horse is bending not leg yielding.
7. Do not overbend the horse's neck or you will get a "neck-in."
8. Coordinate your outside rein and inside leg aids to keep the horse on three tracks.
9. Half-halt periodically to ensure the horse stays in self-carriage.
10. Repeat the 10M circle and start over if the horse loses the movement or has difficulty.
11. See Fig. 17.

SHOULDER-IN

This is a lateral movement in which the horse moves forward with a bending frame making three tracks. It is used to teach the horse engagement and suppleness.

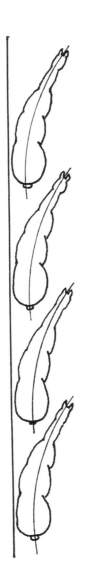

Figure 17

10. DRESSAGE TEST TIPS

A dressage test is performed in a horse show, and SHOW is the operative word. Show off, get out there and strut your stuff. You have paid for seven to eight minutes in that court and it is yours. As previously discussed in the horse psychology section, your attitude plays a big part in the horse's performance. If you are insecure, nervous, and tight, the horse will be too. A positive attitude can really raise those scores.

Being well prepared and having a plan will also help. Here is a good game plan.

1. Know where you want to go.
2. Look where you want to go.
3. Make the horse go there.

KNOW AND LOOK WHERE YOU WANT TO GO

Study the dressage courts in Fig. 18. When riding a dressage test, it is extremely helpful to know your way around the court. Memorize where the letters are, the distances from the corners to the letters, and the distances between letters. The dimensions of the court will help you determine the size of the movements asked for in the test. Every dressage court is exactly the same and is composed of a center line, circles, and diagonals.

The center line is 10M from the side of the court, so the curve at the ends of the center line is a 10M curve (Fig. 20, Pg. 107). Practice 10M circles off the center line and rail so you know how small this movement is. Be sure your aids are appropriate for the amount of bend required for a 10M curve. This ensures that you have the correct bend to hit the center line and not over shoot it.

The diagonal is similar to the center line, but has a 12M curve before and after, because the corner letters (F, K, H, and M) are 6M from the corner (Fig. 21, Pg. 108). This is a straight line; make it straight by correcting the direction of the horse with your leg aids. Use the reins only to keep the horse's head pointed at the letter you are riding to.

The circle seems to be the hardest movement to ride correctly. Riding the horse forward in a correct frame gained from an effective position and use of aids, should produce a round circle. Visual guides will also be helpful. Here are some guides to help you find your way around a circle (study Fig. 19, Pg. 106). Think of the circle as if it were inside a square. The circle will touch the center of each side of the square. Divide the circle into quarters and look ahead one quarter at a time.

For a circle at A or C, the first quarter guide will be on the rail 10M from the end of the court. To determine where this is remember F, K, H, and M are 6M from the corner. The 10M guide on the rail will be 4M (about 12 feet) from the corner letter. Look for this quarter guide on the rail and ride to it.

Now you are headed toward the center line and out in open space. When leaving your first quarter guide on the rail, look for the spot on the center line 2M or about 6 feet outside the line from R to S or V to P. This is the second quarter guide. Recall the distances between letters. R, S, V, and P are 18M from the end of the court. Use these letters to determine the shape of the square, which will be a line across the court 2M (about 6 feet) outside R to S or V to P.

Next look for that spot on the rail 4M from the

corner letter. This is the third quarter guide. For the last quarter guide, look at A or C and make the horse go there.

For a circle at E or B in a long court, use the same guides on the center line. Study Fig. 21 and note that the end and center circles touch on the center line. The center line guides for the circles at E or B will be 2M toward the center from the R to S or V to P lines.

In a short court the circles at A or C will go to X on the center line. The circles at E or B are more difficult in a short court (Fig. 19). The circle will cross the center line 4M or 12 feet inside a line from the corner letters (F, K, H, and M) which is hard to judge. This guide is also half way (10M) from X to the end of the court.

Look ahead and plan ahead. Be well prepared for your next movement before you get to the letter and must depart.

SHORT AND LONG DRESSAGE COURTS

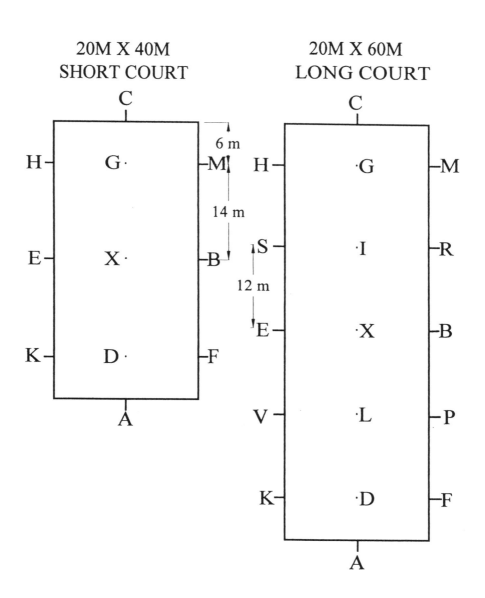

20M X 40M SHORT COURT

20M X 60M LONG COURT

Figure 18

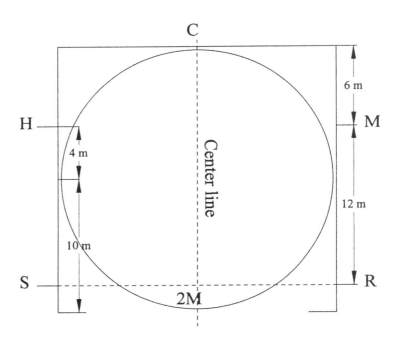

Think of the circle as if it were inside a square. The circle will touch the center of each side of the square. Learn the dimensions of the dressage court and use them to help guide you during the movements in a dressage test.

Figure 19

SHORT COURT MOVEMENTS

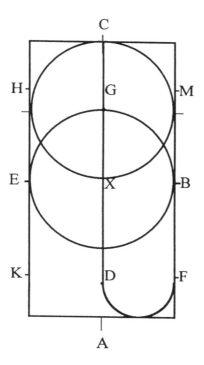

In the short court, a circle at A or C will go to X and back to A or C. Note where the circle touches the rail on the long sides. This guide is approximately twelve feet from the corner letter (F,K,H, or M). The center circle at E or B touches the centerline approximately twelve feet from a line between the corner letters. The turn at the end of the centerline is a 10M half circle.

Try to visualize these movements on the paper and in an empty dressage court. Practice riding these movements combining the feeling of the horse's frame, impulsion, and submission, as well as looking for guides in the dressage court.

Figure 20

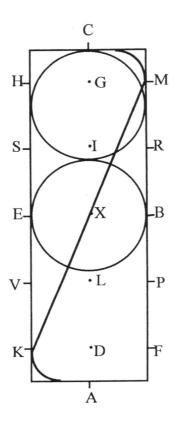

The long court has three circles, two of which, at A and C, are the same. The distance between letters in a long court is 12M instead of 14M as in a short court. The circles at A or C touch the centerline approximately six feet beyond a line between R to S or V to P. The center circle at E or B touches the centerline at the above guide six feet inside a line between R to S or V to P.

Look at the difference in the corner between the depth of the track for a circle and the track for the turn at the end or beginning of a diagonal. The circle corner is a

Figure 21

20M curve and the diagonal corner is a 12M curve, because the corner letter is 6M from the corner. Practice riding each of these tracks with a pattern of diagonal-circle-diagonal-circle. Once again study the movements on the paper and in the dressage court. Know where you want to go and then make the horse go there.

MAKE THE HORSE GO THERE

Now that you know where to go and are going to look there, you are ready to ride the dressage test. Your hand, leg, and seat aids are the navigation tools for controlling and directing the horse. These are some tips to help you ride the three basic movements.

CENTER LINE

1. Ride the horse at a walk in front of the judge's stand. Give the horse a good look with each eye.
2. Plan a good entry giving yourself lots of room for a turn and long, straight entry.
3. Go forward up the center line with your eye glued on C.
4. Prepare far enough ahead for the halt at X.
5. Don't allow the horse to move off from the halt until you finish the salute.
6. Keep the horse's head centered in front of his chest and pointed at C.
7. Use your leg aids (not hands) to correct the horse if he moves off the center line.
8. Prepare well for a bend as you reach the end of the center line. Your aids should be appropriate for a 10M curve.
9. Look for the center line half way through the corner when riding the turn up the center line at the end of your test.
10. Never go over the center line. It is better to turn early than late.
11. Prepare far enough ahead for the halt at the end of your test.

DIAGONALS

1. Prepare the horse well for a good bend in the corner preceding a diagonal and ride a 12M curve.
2. Use the outside rein and your outside leg to take the horse off the rail at the corner letter, which will straighten the horse and send him forward on the diagonal.
3. Keep your eye glued on the letter at the end of the diagonal.
4. Keep the horse's head centered in front of his chest and pointed at the letter at the end of the diagonal.
5. Use your leg aids to correct the horse if he moves off the line.
6. Maintain a steady forward motion and rhythm.
7. Prepare well for a bend as you reach the end of the diagonal. Your aids should be appropriate for a 12M curve.
8. Be ready with your inside leg in case the horse cuts the corner.
9. Use your inside leg to push the horse to the rail at the end of your diagonal and into the corner.

20M CIRCLE

1. Prepare for the bend before starting the circle.
2. Ensure the horse is on the outside rein.
3. Establish a bend and take the horse off the rail with your outside leg to start the circle.
4. Divide the circle in quarters and look ahead at the court for each guide.

5. Use your inside leg or outside leg to keep the horse on the correct track for a round circle.

6. Try to maintain consistent bend, rhythm, and tempo.

7. Push the horse back on the rail at the end of the circle with your inside leg.

8. Ride a tighter corner before and after the diagonal to show the difference in the corner tracks of the circle versus the diagonal.

CONCLUSION

The most important aspect of riding dressage is to have fun with your horse and friends. The true enjoyment of the sport is not just getting great scores and winning ribbons (although it does boost your ego).

My greatest joy is the close relationship and communication I have with my horse. Through dressage, an extraordinary communication level gains trust and confidence, which is enjoyed by both horse and rider. The ability to persuade this magnificent animal to willingly perform the graceful and dynamic movements of dressage, is the ultimate equestrian achievement.